Totally **WACKY**
FACTS ABOUT
YOU!

CARI MEISTER

CAPSTONE PRESS
a capstone imprint

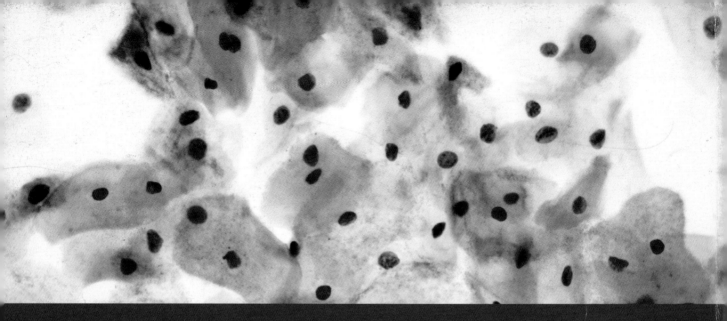

The body has **200** types of cells, including those found in our blood, skin, and muscles.

50–100 TRILLION:
the number of cells in an adult's body

If a cell is damaged or has an infection, it self-destructs!

MUSCLE CELLS LIVE AS LONG AS YOU DO.

Skin cells live for one to 30 days.

WHITE BLOOD CELLS LIVE FOR LESS THAN ONE DAY!

Skin is your body's LARGEST ORGAN.

WITHOUT SKIN YOU WOULD EVAPORATE.

40 POUNDS
(18 KILOGRAMS): THE AMOUNT OF SKIN YOU WILL SHED IN YOUR LIFETIME

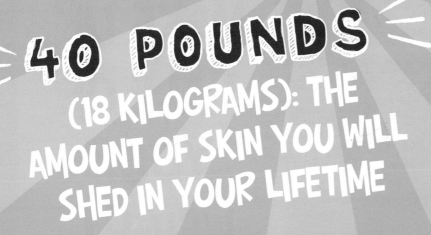

You use 200 muscles to take one step!

MUSCLES MAKE UP HALF OF YOUR WEIGHT.

To kiss, a person uses 34 FACIAL MUSCLES.

9

You have 206 bones in your body—106 of them are in your hands and feet.

YOUR FEMUR (THIGHBONE) IS THE STRONGEST BONE IN YOUR BODY.

Bones are stronger than concrete!

THE AVERAGE NUMBER OF BROKEN BONES A PERSON HAS IN A LIFETIME IS TWO.

Want to keep your bones strong? Drink more MILK!

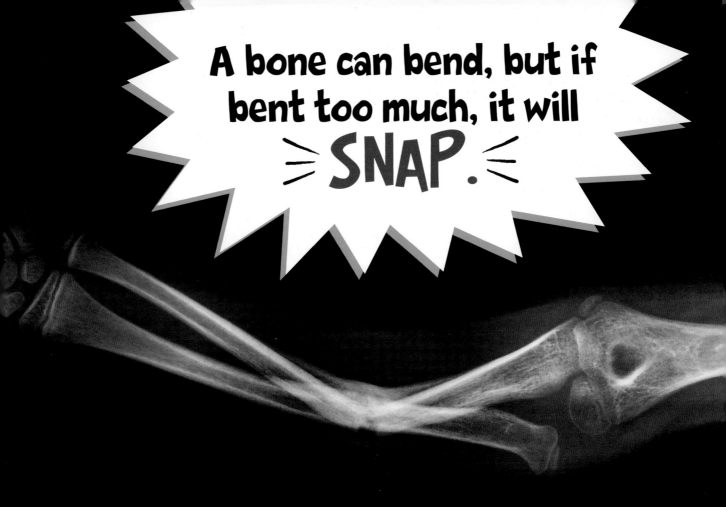

A bone can bend, but if bent too much, it will ≳ SNAP. ≲

Your teeth are the only bones that can't repair themselves.

Your baby teeth grew before you were born—they were just hiding beneath your gums.

ABOUT ONE BABY IN 2,500 IS BORN WITH A TOOTH SHOWING.

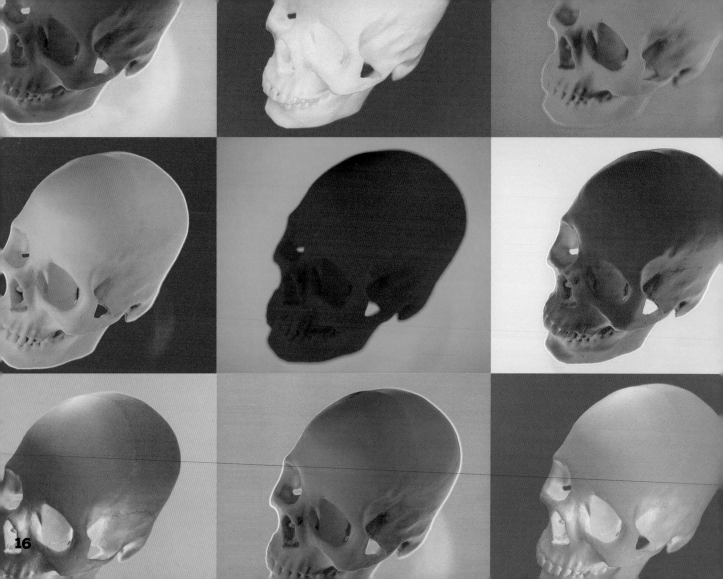

AN ADULT'S SKULL IS MADE UP OF 22 BONES.

Your brain is active while YOU SLEEP.

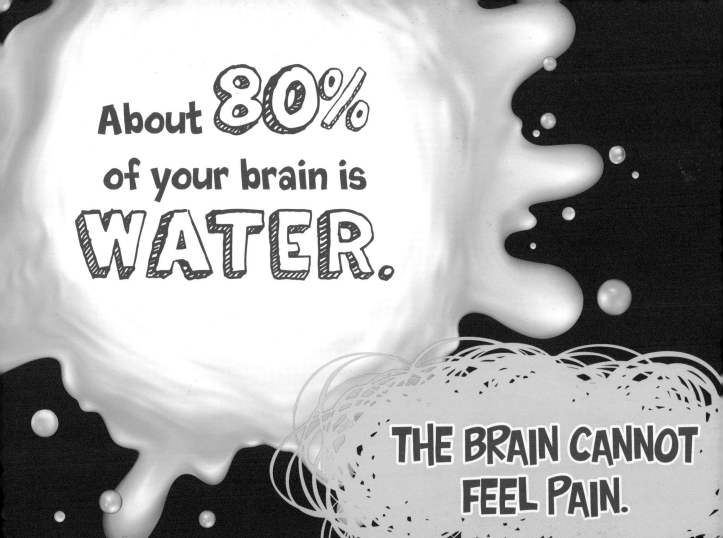

About 80% of your brain is WATER.

THE BRAIN CANNOT FEEL PAIN.

THE NERVOUS SYSTEM IS BASICALLY THE BODY'S ELECTRICAL WIRING.

Neurons send signals through the nervous system that travel at about 328 feet (100 meters) per second!

Your brain has about 100 billion neurons in it!

A human has a **LENS** that works very much like a **CAMERA LENS.**

Your **EYES** are made mostly of a jelly-like goop.

YOU BLINK ABOUT 6,205,000 TIMES IN ONE YEAR!

23

SOME PEOPLE CAN HEAR THEIR EYEBALLS MOVING.

EXOPHTHALMOS IS A CONDITION IN WHICH A PERSON'S EYEBALLS BULGE.

SOME PEOPLE ARE BORN WITHOUT IRISES—THE COLORED PARTS OF THE EYES.

ALMOST ALL ADULTS HAVE **MITES** LIVING ON THEIR EYELASHES.

MITES

Some people have two rows of EYELASHES.

YOUR THUMB IS THE SAME SIZE AS THE LENGTH OF YOUR NOSE.

Your ears and nose never stop growing.

YOUR NOSE IS MADE OF CARTILAGE—THE SAME STUFF THAT MAKES UP A SHARK'S SKELETON.

60% OF MEN OVER AGE 60 SNORE.

Less than 2 % of people in the world have red hair.

YOUR HAIR IS DEAD. THAT'S WHY IT DOESN'T HURT WHEN YOU CUT IT.

Hypertrichosis
(werewolf syndrome)
causes abnormal hair growth
all over the body.

People with
alopecia universalis
cannot grow
hair anywhere.

BLONDES HAVE MORE HAIR THAN PEOPLE WITH OTHER HAIR COLORS.

EVERY DAY YOU LOSE ABOUT 75 STRANDS OF HAIR.

LIPS DO NOT SWEAT.

YOUR LIPS GET THINNER AS YOU GET OLDER.

Very thin skin covers lips.
The blood underneath the skin
makes lips look red!

YOUR TONGUE IS ONE OF THE STRONGEST MUSCLES IN YOUR BODY.

The longest tongue ever recorded was 3.97 inches (10 centimeters).

EVERY TONGUE PRINT IS UNIQUE.

No one is exactly sure why we yawn.

People yawn more during winter.

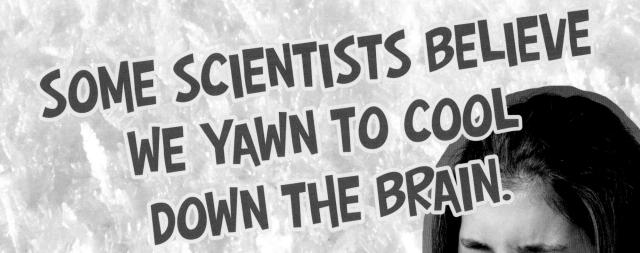

SOME SCIENTISTS BELIEVE WE YAWN TO COOL DOWN THE BRAIN.

Most yawns last about 6 seconds.

43

YOU HAVE ABOUT **9,000** TASTE BUDS ON YOUR **TONGUE.**

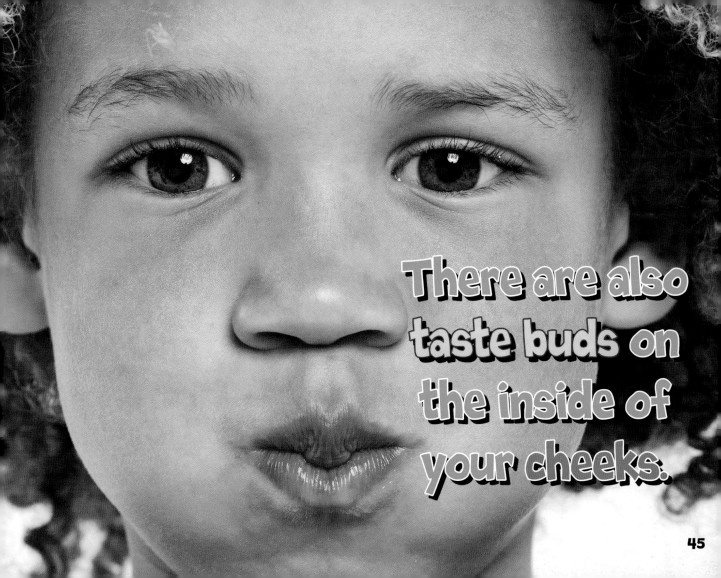

There are also taste buds on the inside of your cheeks.

A sneeze can travel up to **100 miles per hour** (161 kilometers per hour).

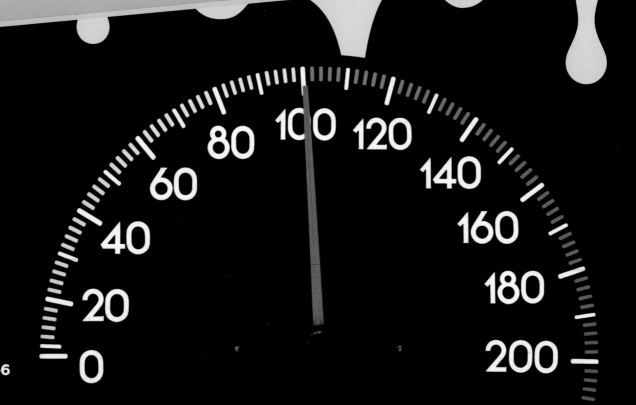

Donna Griffiths, a **12-YEAR-OLD** from England, sneezed for **978** days in a row!

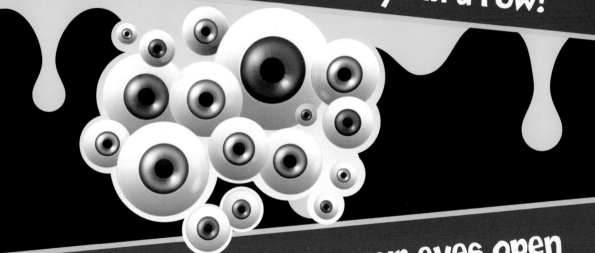

It is impossible to keep your eyes open when you sneeze.

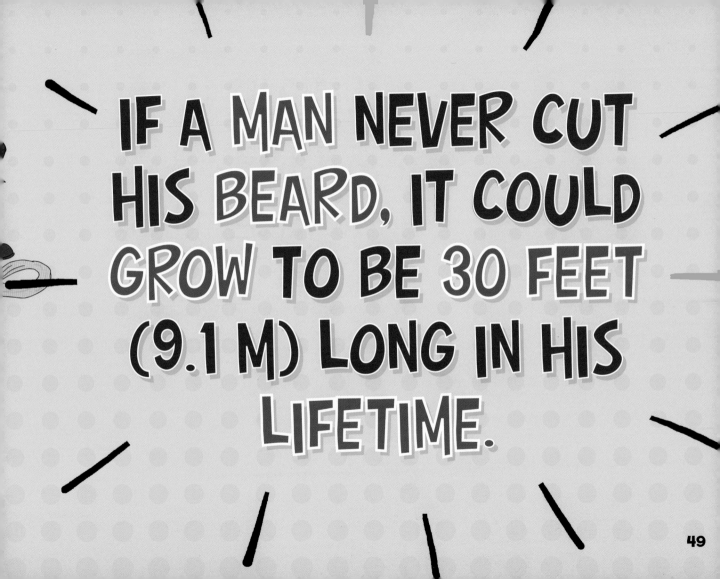

IF A MAN NEVER CUT HIS BEARD, IT COULD GROW TO BE 30 FEET (9.1 M) LONG IN HIS LIFETIME.

WHEN YOU'RE SCARED, YOUR EARS MAKE EXTRA EARWAX.

Earwax is not really wax. It's a mix of oil, sweat, hair, and dead skin.

SOME PEOPLE BELIEVE THAT IF YOU HAVE STICKY EARWAX, YOU STINK!

AN AVERAGE HUMAN HEART WILL BEAT ABOUT

2.5 BILLION

TIMES IN A **LIFETIME.**

A heart can beat outside of a body for a short time.

YOUR HEART ISN'T REALLY RED. IT'S A **RED-BROWN** COLOR WITH PATCHES OF **YELLOW FAT**.

53

YOUR BODY CONTAINS ABOUT 60,000 MILES (96,561 KM) OF BLOOD VESSELS!

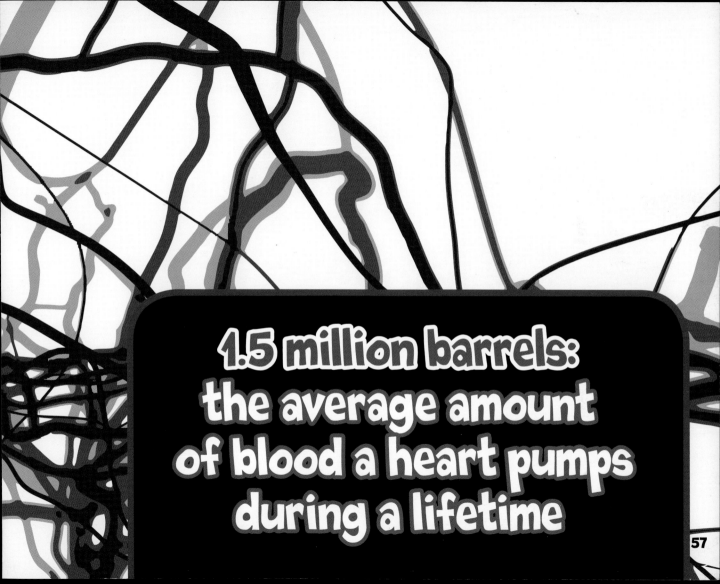

1.5 million barrels:
the average amount
of blood a heart pumps
during a lifetime

You have about **25 TRILLION** red blood cells.

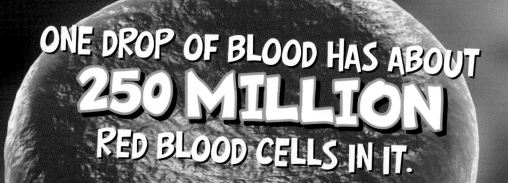

ONE DROP OF BLOOD HAS ABOUT
250 MILLION
RED BLOOD CELLS IN IT.

SOME PEOPLE CAN PLAY THE PIANO WITH THEIR TOES.

More than half of the world's population has one foot that is bigger than the other.

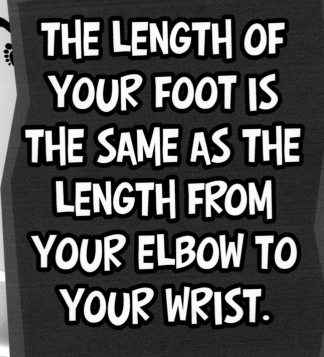

THE LENGTH OF YOUR FOOT IS THE SAME AS THE LENGTH FROM YOUR ELBOW TO YOUR WRIST.

Pig and **cow** heart valves can be used to replace bad heart valves in humans.

If you lose a finger, a toe can be sewn on to replace it.

Fingernails grow about **3 TO 4 TIMES** faster than toenails.

IF YOU LOSE A TOENAIL, IT MAY TAKE ONE YEAR FOR IT TO GROW BACK.

Nails curl when you let them grow very long.

MILLIONS OF TEENY, TINY CREATURES LIVE BENEATH YOUR NAILS.

65

You are tallest in the morning, because gravity pulls downward on your body throughout the day.

THE TALLEST MAN EVER WAS ROBERT WADLOW. HE MEASURED 8 FEET, 11 INCHES (2.7 METERS) TALL.

ASTRONAUTS

ARE 2 INCHES (5.08 CM) TALLER WHILE THEY ARE IN

SPACE.

LUNGS ARE SPONGY.

The left lung is smaller than the right lung.

The average person takes about 7 million breaths in one year.

YOU HAVE
1,000 MILES (1,609 KM)
OF AIRWAYS
IN YOUR BODY.

Sweat is like air-conditioning for your body.

Sweat doesn't smell. It's the bacteria that live near the sweat glands that stink.

70

MOST PEOPLE SWEAT ABOUT 278 GALLONS (1,052 LITERS) PER YEAR.

THERE ARE 500,000 SWEAT GLANDS IN YOUR FEET.

STRESSED OUT?

Your body makes a hormone called adrenaline when you're under stress.

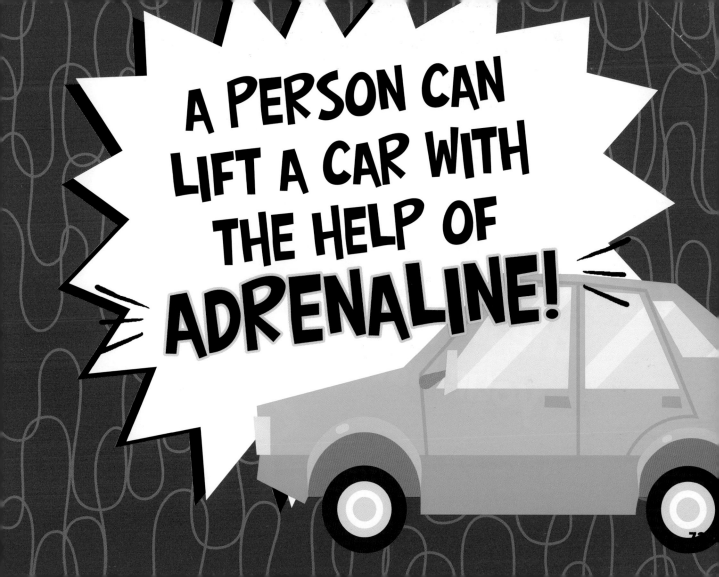

Your kidneys look like giant kidney beans. They're about 4 inches (10 cm) long, or about the length of your hand.

KIDNEYS FILTER ABOUT 50 GALLONS (189 L) OF BLOOD PER DAY. THAT'S ENOUGH TO FILL A LARGE TRASH CAN!

YOUR SPLEEN IS SOFT AND **PURPLE** AND IS ABOUT THE SIZE OF YOUR **FIST.**

YOU CAN LIVE WITHOUT YOUR SPLEEN.

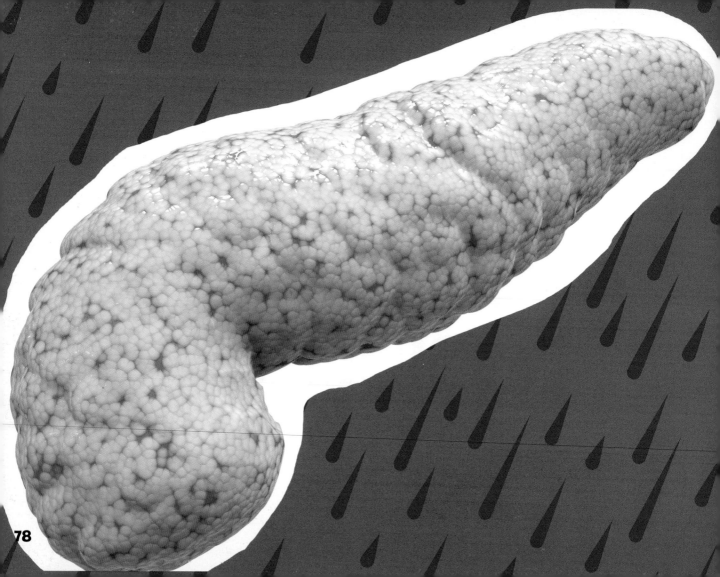

78

A PANCREAS IS SHAPED KIND OF LIKE A SKINNY SOCK.

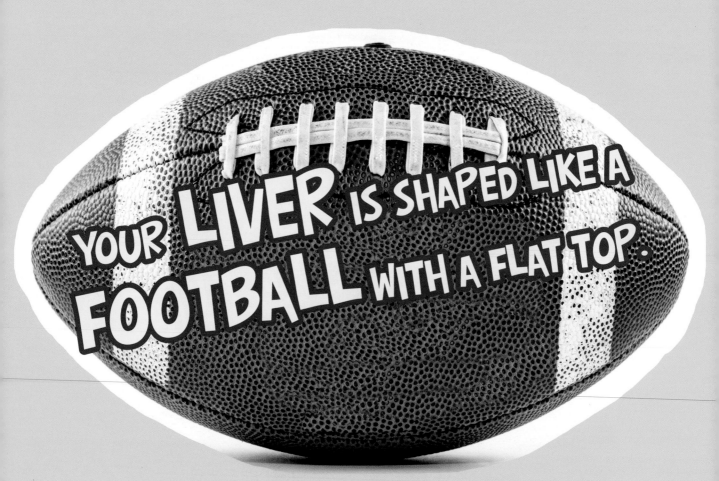

YOUR **LIVER** IS SHAPED LIKE A **FOOTBALL** WITH A FLAT TOP.

At **3½ POUNDS** (1.6 kg), the liver wins the title for the heaviest internal organ.

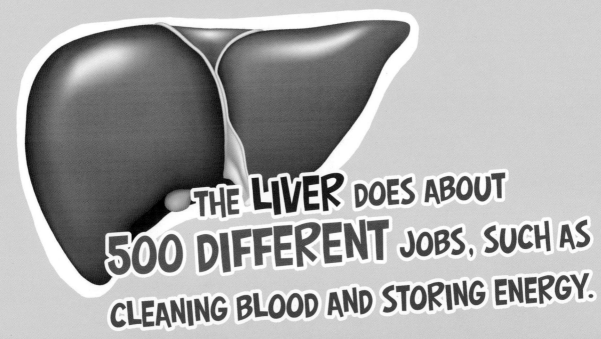

THE **LIVER** DOES ABOUT **500 DIFFERENT** JOBS, SUCH AS CLEANING BLOOD AND STORING ENERGY.

BILE IS BITTER.
YOU CAN TASTE IT
WHEN YOU VOMIT.

YOUR **BELLYBUTTON** IS REALLY A SCAR WHERE YOUR UMBILICAL CORD WAS CUT.

THINK YOU'RE CLEAN?

MANY DIFFERENT KINDS OF BACTERIA LIVE INSIDE YOUR BELLYBUTTON!

YOU CAN LIVE ABOUT ONE WEEK WITHOUT WATER.

A PERSON CAN LIVE UP TO TWO MONTHS WITHOUT FOOD.

THE FOOD YOU EAT SPENDS ABOUT 2 TO 4 HOURS IN YOUR STOMACH.

Your stomach is full of acid. It's what breaks down your food.

THE ACID IN YOUR STOMACH IS SO STRONG IT CAN DISSOLVE METAL!

IF COMPLETELY UNCOILED, YOUR INTESTINES WOULD BE ABOUT 25 FEET (7.62 M) LONG.

THAT'S ABOUT AS LONG

AS AN ORCA WHALE.

DID YOU KNOW THAT POOP CAN BE PURPLE OR BLUE?

You will poop about **7 TONS** (6.4 metric tons) in your lifetime.

The bladder is a bag made out of STRETCHY MUSCLE.

WHEN YOUR BLADDER IS FULL, IT IS THE SIZE OF A GRAPEFRUIT.

You may have **6 BILLION** bacteria living in your mouth.

Some **BACTERIA** help you to digest foods. Other bacteria help protect your gums.

3 TO 5 POUNDS (1.36 TO 2.27 KG):
THE AMOUNT OF BACTERIA THE AVERAGE PERSON CARRIES

EVERYBODY FARTS!
SOME PEOPLE JUST DON'T ADMIT IT.

SODA AND GUM
CAN MAKE YOU FART MORE.

Some people eat their HAIR.

THE LARGEST HAIR BALL REMOVED FROM A PERSON'S STOMACH WEIGHED 10 POUNDS (4.54 KG)!

YOU PROBABLY HAVE ENOUGH
FAT IN YOUR
BODY TO MAKE ABOUT
75 CANDLES.

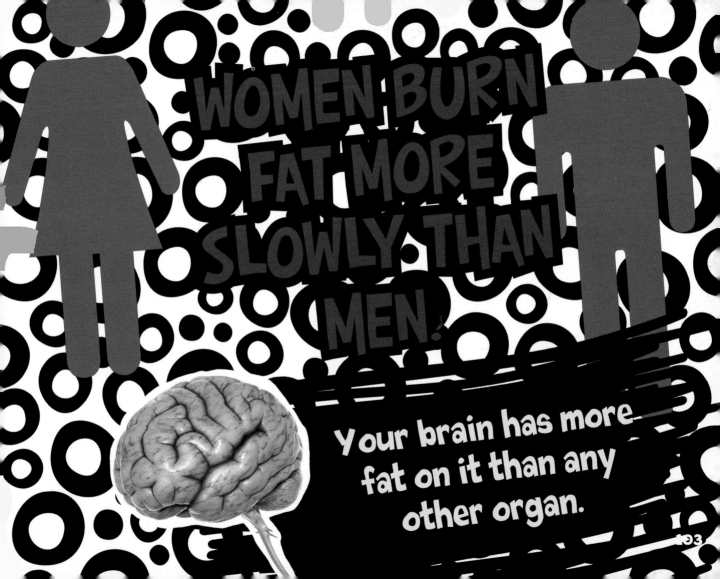

YOUR BODY MAKES ABOUT **3 SODA CANS** WORTH OF **PHLEGM** AND **MUCUS** PER DAY.

BURP! THAT'S THE SOUND OF GAS MAKING YOUR ESOPHAGUS VIBRATE.

THE **LOUDEST BURP** RECORDED WAS 118.1 DECIBELS—ABOUT AS LOUD AS A PLANE TAKING OFF!

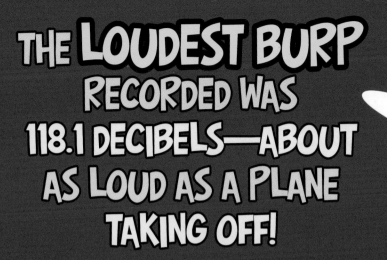

The faster you eat, the more gas you will have.

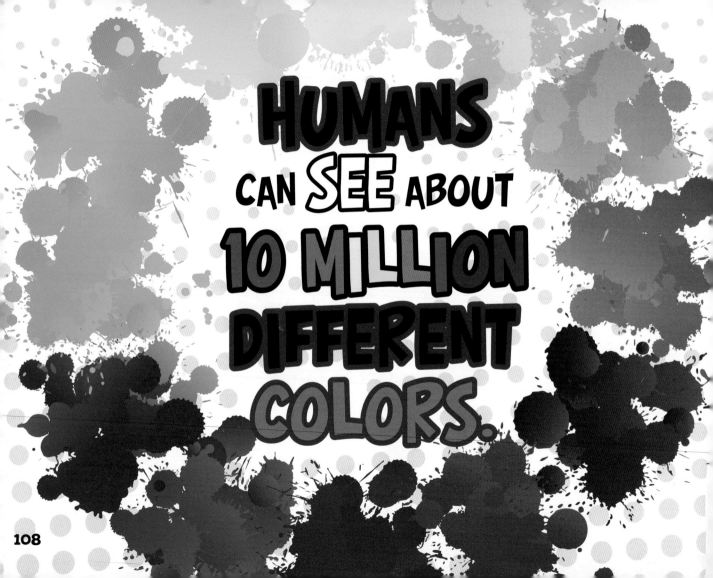

HUMANS CAN SEE ABOUT 10 MILLION DIFFERENT COLORS.

WE **HEAR** THINGS WHILE WE SLEEP, BUT OUR BRAINS DON'T DETECT THE SOUNDS.

THE NOSE CAN DETECT ABOUT 1 TRILLION DIFFERENT SMELLS.

Your **mouth** makes about
4 TO 8 CUPS
(0.9 to 1.9 l)
of **saliva** per day!

An adult pees about 6 cups (1.4 l) per day.

Some foods, like asparagus, can make your urine smell strange.

THE TIP OF YOUR NOSE AND YOUR EARS ARE MADE UP OF CARTILAGE.

Cartilage is also found between bones. It keeps them from rubbing together.

THE CARTILAGE IN YOUR JOINTS CAN SOAK UP WATER BETTER THAN A SPONGE!

A ONE-TIME *Blood* DONOR CAN SAVE THE LIVES OF UP TO 3 PEOPLE.

THE BRAIN IS LIKE MISSION CONTROL FOR THE ENTIRE BODY.

YOU CAN'T DANCE WITHOUT YOUR BRAIN.

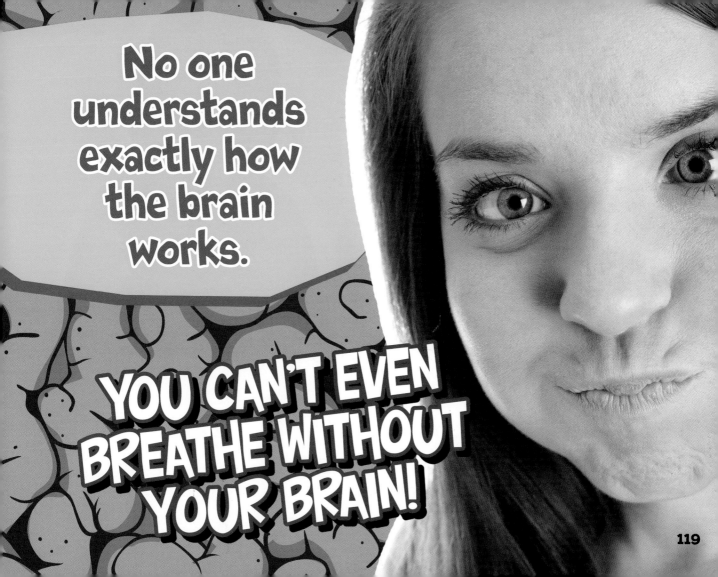

119

A BABY'S SKULL IS PARTLY OPEN TO MAKE ROOM FOR ITS BRAIN (AND MIND) TO GROW.

A baby's brain doubles in size in the first year.

At 1 year old, a baby's brain is about **60%** of its adult size.

BY AGE 5 A CHILD'S BRAIN HAS REACHED ITS FULL SIZE!

LEARNING NEW THINGS HELPS YOUR BRAIN GROW.

A 3-YEAR-OLD'S BRAIN IS $2\frac{1}{2}$ TIMES MORE ACTIVE THAN AN ADULT'S BRAIN.

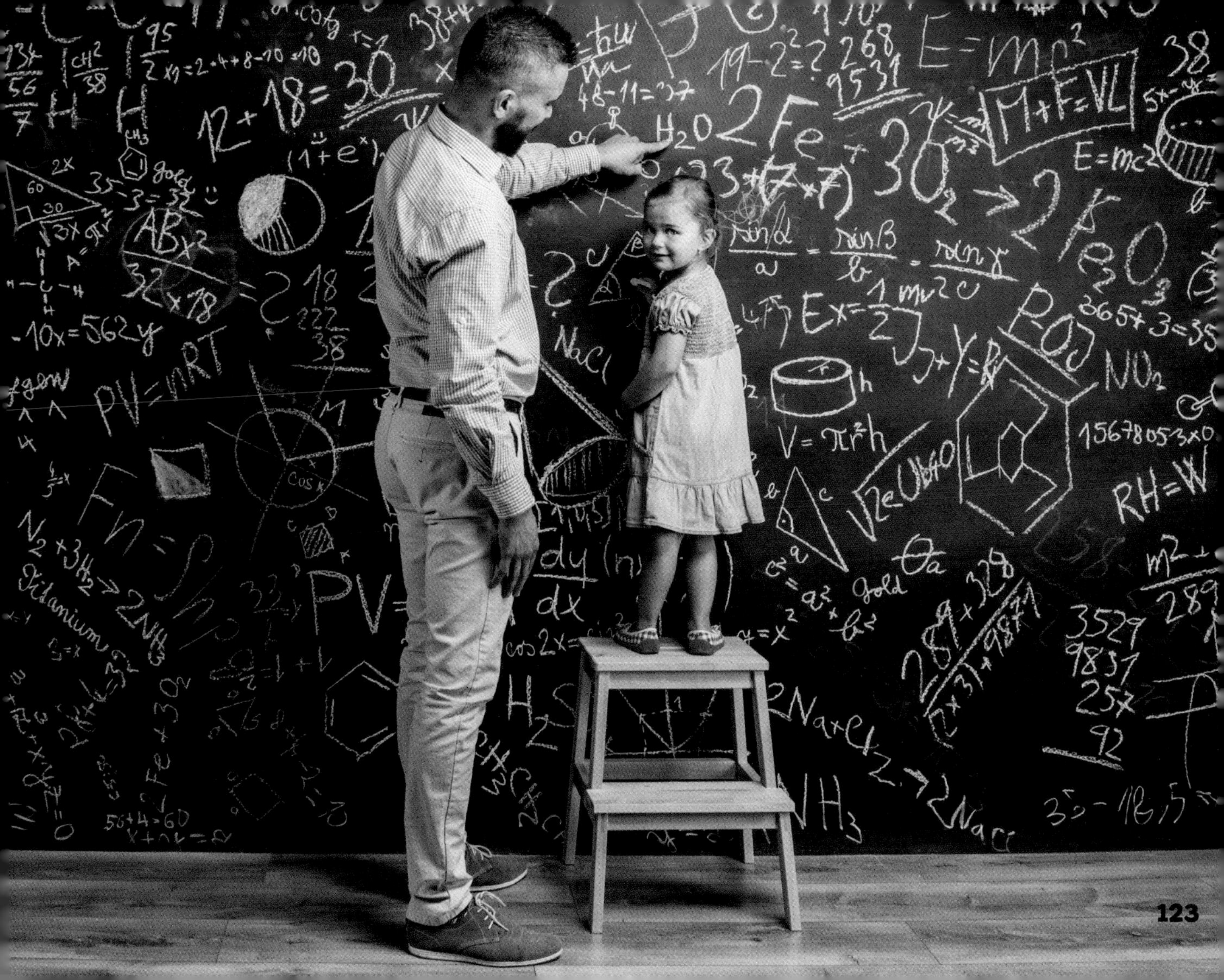

E=mc2
12+18=30
H2O
PV=nRT
NaCl
NO2
V=πr2h
RH=W
gold
Titanium

ONE STUDY SAYS THE BRAINS OF MEN AND WOMEN ARE WIRED DIFFERENTLY.

Women and men use different brain parts to do the same activities.

GIRLS' BRAINS MATURE FASTER THAN BOYS' BRAINS.

THE AVERAGE BRAIN WEIGHS ABOUT ≥ 3 POUNDS ≤ (1.36 KILOGRAMS) AND IS THE SIZE OF A CANTALOUPE.

ON AVERAGE, MEN HAVE BIGGER BRAINS THAN WOMEN.

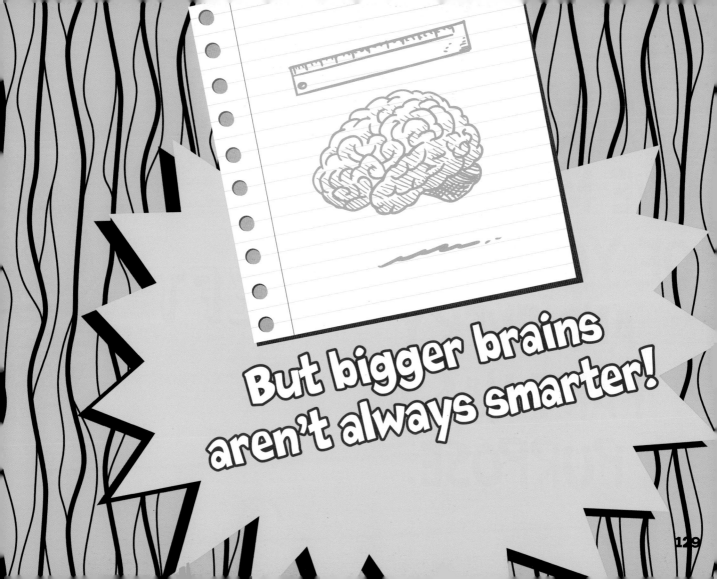

But bigger brains aren't always smarter!

THERE ARE FIVE MAIN PARTS OF YOUR BRAIN, AND EVERY PART HAS A PURPOSE.

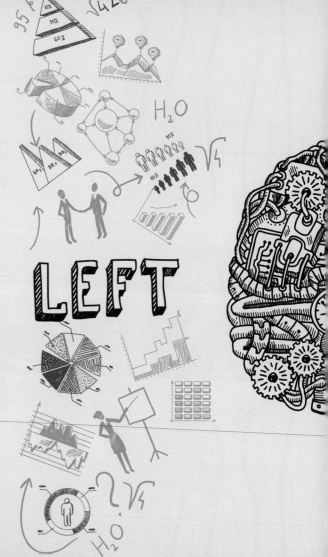

EACH SIDE OF YOUR BRAIN CONTROLS THE OPPOSITE SIDE OF YOUR BODY.

YOU ARE LEAVING

PAIN

ENJOY THE JOURNEY!

The BRAIN itself does not feel PAIN.

There's a thermometer in your head—the **hypothalamus!**

THE PEARL-SIZED PART CONTROLS YOUR TEMPERATURE.

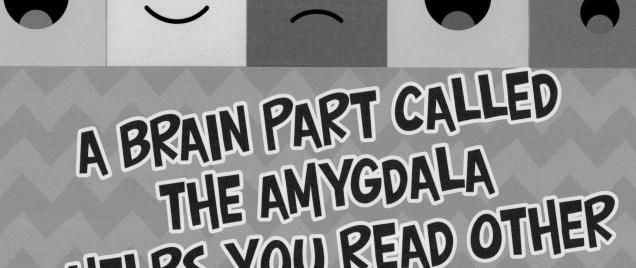

A BRAIN PART CALLED THE AMYGDALA HELPS YOU READ OTHER PEOPLE'S EMOTIONS.

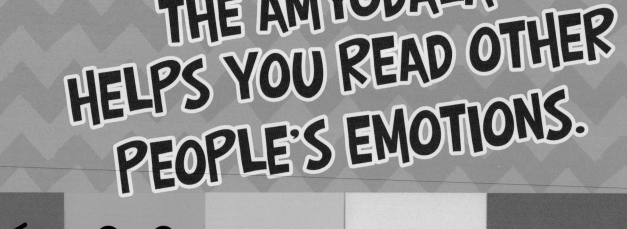

It's also the part that tells you to **SCREAM** when you're scared!

Like monarch butterflies, humans may have an internal compass.

CAN WE TRAVEL ACROSS THE GLOBE WITHOUT HELP FROM A MAP?

YOUR BRAIN FEELS KIND OF LIKE SLIMY GELATIN.

Part of your brain looks wrinkly.

Your brain has a stem.

Your skull is like a **HELMET** for your **BRAIN.**

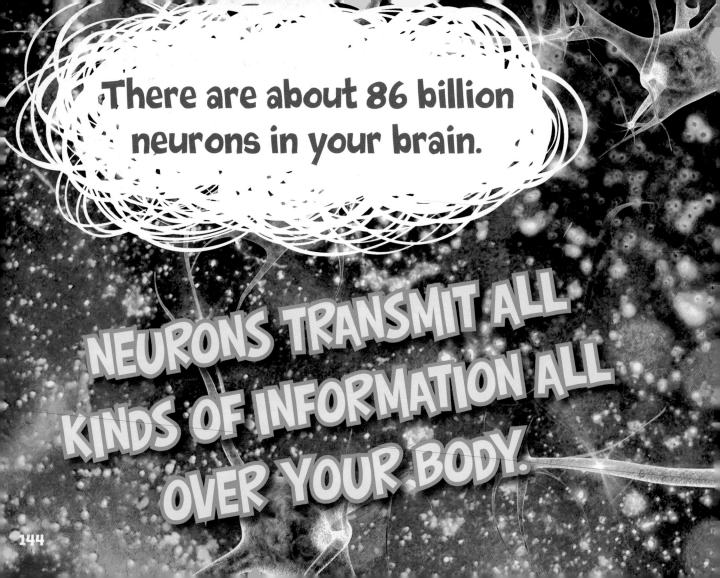

There are about 86 billion neurons in your brain.

NEURONS TRANSMIT ALL KINDS OF INFORMATION ALL OVER YOUR BODY.

It would take you more than three years to count all your neurons!

You have about

100,000 MILES

(160,934 km)

of blood vessels
in your brain.

EVERY MINUTE ABOUT THREE SODA CANS WORTH OF BLOOD FLOW TO THE BRAIN.

YOUR BRAIN MAKES ENOUGH ENERGY TO POWER A LIGHTBULB.

The outside of your brain is pink.

Parts of the brain are white.

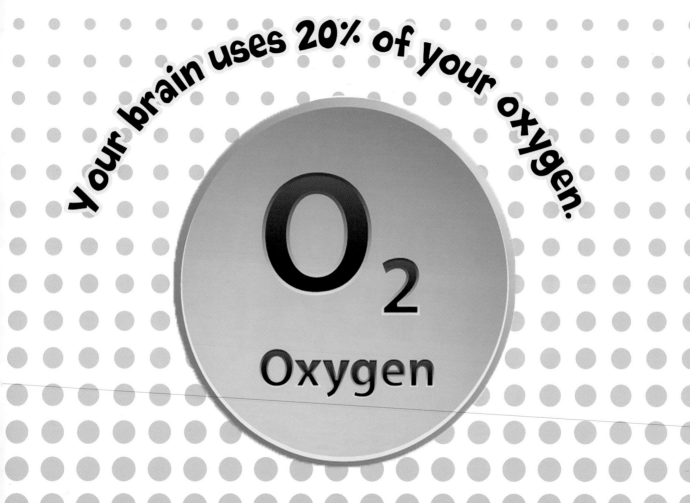

Your brain uses 20% of your oxygen.

O$_2$

Oxygen

4 TO 6 MINUTES: THE AMOUNT OF TIME YOUR BRAIN CAN LIVE WITHOUT OXYGEN

YOU CAN FUNCTION WITH HALF A BRAIN.

THE UNITED STATES HAS PERFORMED MORE LOBOTOMIES THAN ANY OTHER COUNTRY.

60% OF YOUR BRAIN IS FAT.

Your brain will eat itself if your diet is missing important nutrients.

IT'S A MYTH THAT WE USE ONLY 10% OF OUR BRAIN.

Throughout a single day, we actually use all parts of the brain.

BRAINS HAVE NOT BEEN TRANSPLANTED YET, BUT SOME DAY THEY COULD BE!

WHEN YOU DIE, YOU CAN DONATE YOUR BRAIN TO SCIENCE.

HARVARD UNIVERSITY KEEPS A BRAIN BANK OF ABOUT 3,000 BRAINS.

Your brain can process information very quickly—about 268 miles (431 km) per hour.

Your body can sense **11 MILLION** bits of information per second.

You can process only about **40** of them.

YOU HAVE ABOUT 70,000 THOUGHTS PER DAY.

DAYDREAMING IS GOOD FOR YOUR MIND.

The average person daydreams about 47% of the day.

Daydreaming helps your brain make new connections.

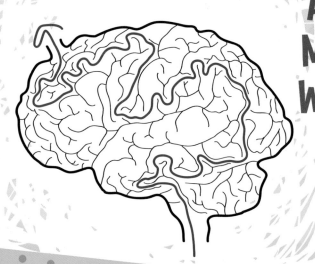

A PHYSICAL PATH IS MADE IN YOUR BRAIN WHENEVER YOU HAVE A THOUGHT.

The more times you have had a thought, the easier it is to have again.

THINK GOOD THOUGHTS! IT WILL MAKE YOU A HAPPIER PERSON.

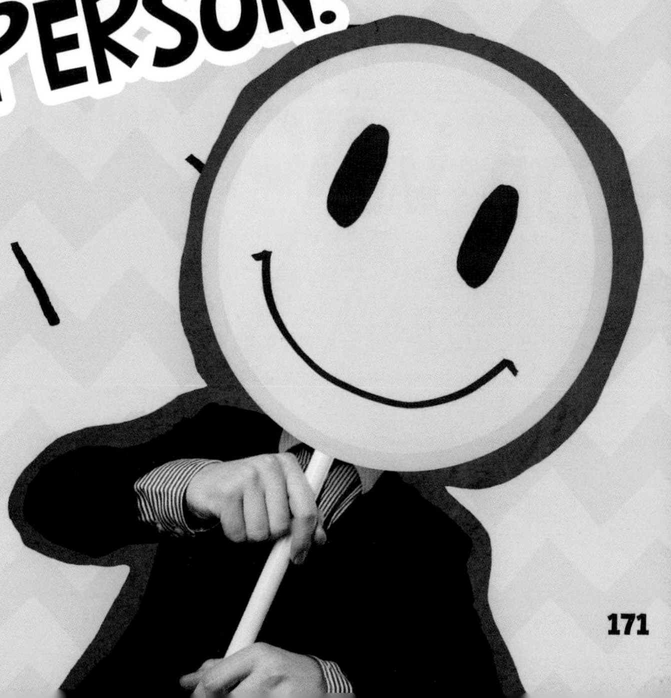

Only about **10%** of the population is left-handed.

MICHELANGELO AND DA VINCI WERE LEFT-HANDED.

A STUDY SAYS THAT LEFT-HANDERS DO BETTER ON HIGH-STAKES TESTS.

It also said that lefties get scared more easily than righties.

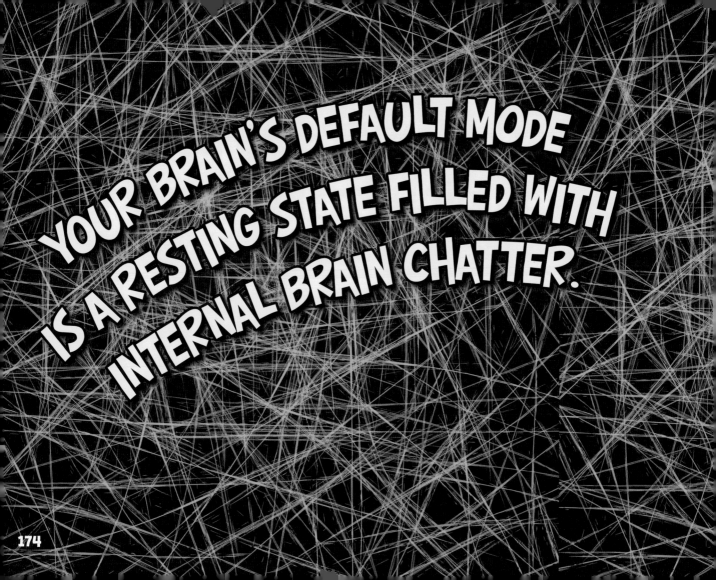

YOUR BRAIN'S DEFAULT MODE IS A RESTING STATE FILLED WITH INTERNAL BRAIN CHATTER.

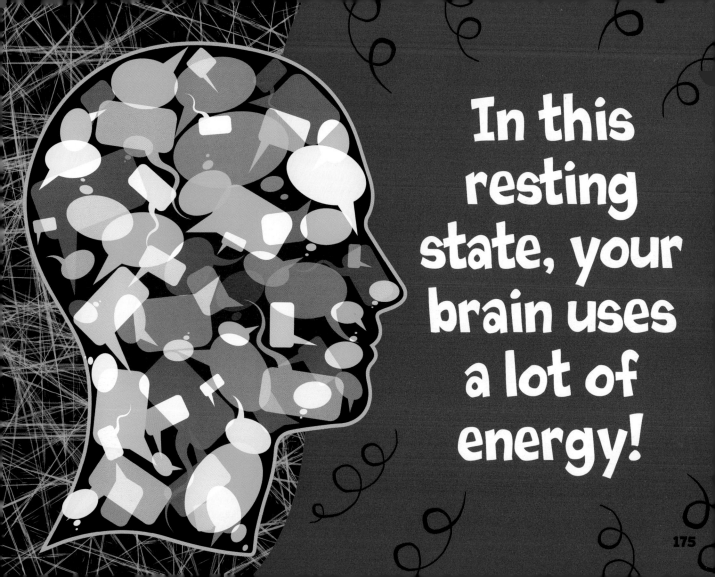

In this resting state, your brain uses a lot of energy!

175

YOUR MEMORY OF SOMETHING IS OFTEN WRONG.

Things we see all the time can be easily forgotten because we see them so often.

Your brain changes your memories when you talk about them.

SOME PEOPLE BELIEVE THEIR MINDS CAN PREDICT THE FUTURE. THEY'RE CALLED CLAIRVOYANTS.

IF SOMEONE IS BELIEVED TO BE **TELEPATHIC**, HE OR SHE CAN POSSIBLY READ SOMEONE ELSE'S MIND.

ESP stands for "extra sensory perception."

PEOPLE WHO THINK THEY HAVE ESP BELIEVE THEY CAN SENSE THINGS WITH THEIR MINDS.

CRIME INVESTIGATORS SOMETIMES ASK SOMEONE WITH ESP TO HELP SOLVE A CASE.

Déjà vu is kind of like a brain hiccup. It happens when there is a brain malfunction.

SOME PEOPLE BELIEVE DÉJÀ VU HAPPENS WHEN TWO UNIVERSES COLLIDE.

DÉJÀ VU MEANS "ALREADY SEEN" IN FRENCH.

Jigsaw puzzles

exercise parts of the brain.

THERE IS NO SUCH THING AS A TRULY PHOTOGRAPHIC MEMORY.

Some people can memorize
the order of a deck of cards
in under one minute.

A

COLORS CAN INSPIRE OUR BRAINS TO THINK IN A CERTAIN WAY.

The color blue sparks **CREATIVITY**.

The color green makes people feel relaxed.

A TEENAGER NEEDS 9 1/4 HOURS OF SLEEP FOR HIS BRAIN TO FUNCTION PROPERLY.

If you get good sleep, you will get better grades.

MOST TEENAGERS IN THE UNITED STATES DON'T GET ENOUGH SLEEP.

Some people say you can't DREAM and SNORE at the same time.

NUMBER OF DREAMS IN A LIFETIME:

100,000

EVERYONE DREAMS. YOU JUST FORGET MOST OF YOUR DREAMS.

People who are blind dream.

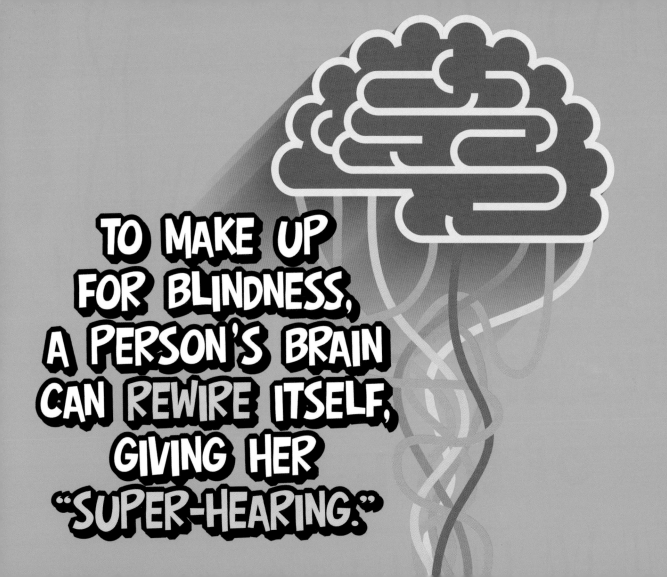

TO MAKE UP FOR BLINDNESS, A PERSON'S BRAIN CAN REWIRE ITSELF, GIVING HER "SUPER-HEARING."

REAL LAUGHTER HAPPENS UNCONSCIOUSLY.

Laughter activates five different parts of the brain.

IN CREATIVE THINKING, THERE IS NEVER ONE ANSWER.

To be creative, you must practice being creative.

A recent study found there is a network over a large area of the brain that is used during creative thinking.

A SCORE OF 100 ON AN IQ TEST MEANS AVERAGE INTELLIGENCE.

Many people do not believe IQ tests actually test overall intelligence.

HIGHEST ADULT IQ ON RECORD: 198

MUSIC CAN HEAL THE BRAIN.

MUSIC HELPS PEOPLE FEEL POSITIVE.

MUSIC CAN REDUCE PAIN.

Music can transport your mind back in time.

Musical training helps some children improve their reading.

PARTS OF YOUR BRAIN ARE ACTIVATED ONLY WHEN PLAYING AN INSTRUMENT.

KNITTING IS GOOD FOR YOUR BRAIN. IT REDUCES STRESS AND ANXIETY.

LIKE PUZZLES, BRAIN GAMES HELP TO IMPROVE YOUR ABILITY TO REASON.

OPTICAL ILLUSIONS TRICK THE BRAIN.

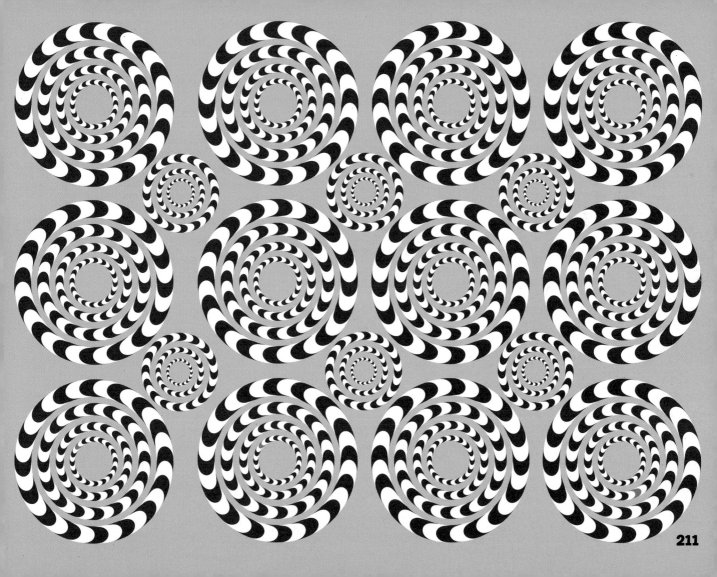

211

Reading to kids makes them smarter.

If you read 20 minutes a day, you will be exposed to 1.8 million words per year!

People who read for fun do better in school.

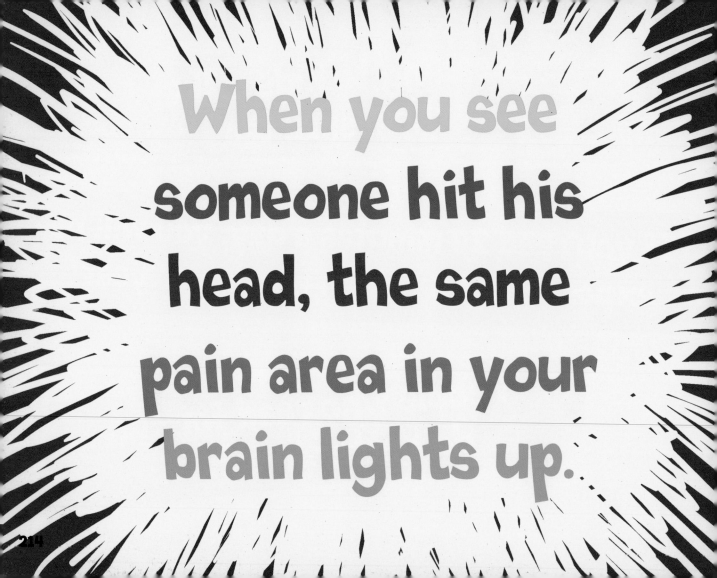

When you see someone hit his head, the same pain area in your brain lights up.

214

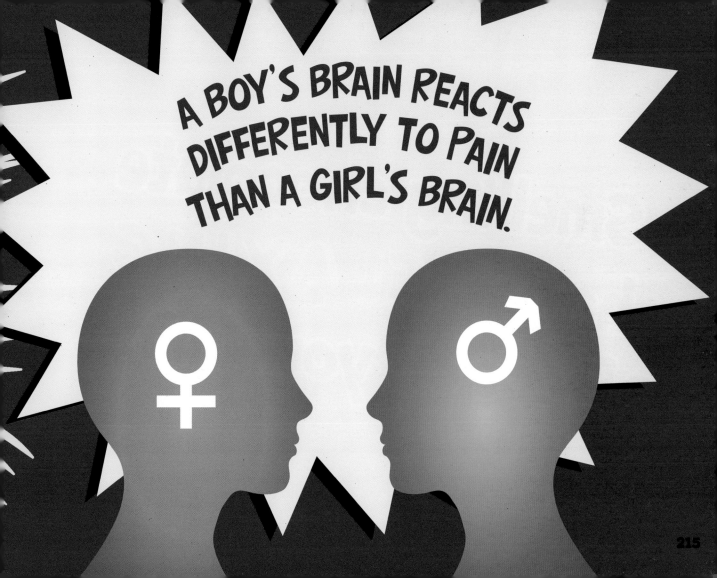

Smelling chocolate has a RELAXING effect on your mind.

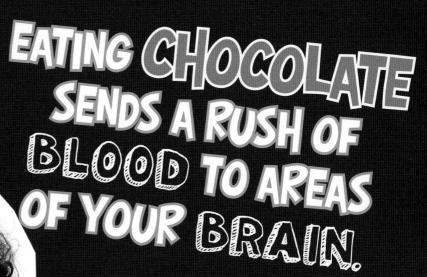

EATING **CHOCOLATE** SENDS A RUSH OF **BLOOD** TO AREAS OF YOUR **BRAIN.**

ONE THEORY SAYS THAT EATING FOODS WITH ARTIFICIAL COLORS SLOWS DOWN YOUR THINKING.

218

Highly processed foods trick your brain into wanting more.

The best foods for your brain: blueberries, avocados, nuts, and seeds

ABOUT 90% OF SICKNESS AND DISEASE IS RELATED TO STRESS IN YOUR MIND.

BEING PHYSICALLY FIT HELPS YOUR BRAIN STAY YOUNG.

You think more clearly after exercising.

Ways to boost your brainpower:

EXERCISE EVERY DAY.

SLEEP WELL.

KEEP LEARNING.

Within 10 minutes of waking from a dream, you forget 90% of what you dreamed.

JAPANESE RESEARCHERS ARE WORKING ON A WAY TO PUT DREAMS ON A SCREEN.

IT'S VERY COMMON TO DREAM ABOUT ALL OF YOUR TEETH FALLING OUT.

THINK YOU HAVE A GREAT MEMORY? DANIEL TAMMENT FROM THE UNITED KINGDOM CAN LEARN AN ENTIRE LANGUAGE IN ABOUT THREE DAYS!

ACRONYMS, SONGS, AND RHYMES HELP US TO MEMORIZE THINGS.

People who have incredible memories often have "malfunctions" in their brains.

SUNSHINE MAKES PEOPLE FEEL HAPPY!

Ever had part of a song stuck in your head? It's called an earworm.

Want to get it out of your head?

Read a book!

GLOSSARY

amygdala—small groups of cells in your brain that are responsible for your feelings

anxiety—a feeling of worry or fear

bacteria—very small living things that exist all around you and inside you; some bacteria cause disease

bile—a green liquid made by the liver that helps digest food

cell—a basic part of an animal or plant that is so small you can't see it without a microscope

detect—to notice something; your sense organs detect things about your surroundings

esophagus—the tube that carries food from the mouth to the stomach; muscles in the esophagus push food into the stomach

filter—to remove unwanted materials

gland—an organ in the body that makes natural chemicals or helps substances leave the body

heart valve—part of the heart that opens and closes to let blood go in and come out

hormone—a chemical made by a gland in the body that affects a person's growth and development

hypothalamus—your brain's thermostat

IQ—short for intelligence quotient; a number used to measure someone's intelligence

liver—the organ responsible for making bile and storing body oils; the liver cleans blood and aids in digestion

lobotomy—a surgical operation on the brain

mature—having reached full growth or development

neuron—a nerve cell

optical illusion—something that makes us see things that do not exist or are different than they appear

organ—a part of the body that does a certain job; your heart, lungs, and kidneys are organs

pancreas—an organ near the stomach that makes insulin

photographic memory—memory that is capable of retaining information that is as clear as a photograph

process—put through a series of tasks

spleen—an organ that is part of the immune system and helps to remove blood cells

theory—an idea that explains something that is unknown

transplant—to remove and replace with one that works

transport—to move from one place to another

umbilical cord—the tube that connects an unborn baby to its mother

ABOUT THE AUTHOR

Cari Meister has written more than a hundred books for children, including the "Tiny" series (Penguin) and the "Meet the Monsters" series (Stone Arch Books). She has received many awards for her books. Most recently, "Airplane Adventure" (Stone Arch Books), was named to "Parents" magazine Best Books for 2010. Today, Cari lives in the mountains of Colorado, with her husband, four boys, two horses, and one dog.

LOOKING FOR MORE TOTALLY WACKY TRIVIA?

237

INDEX

Mind Benders are published by Capstone,
1710 Roe Crest Drive, North Mankato, Minnesota 56003
www.mycapstone.com

Editor: Shelly Lyons
Designer: Lori Bye
Media Researcher: Jo Miller
Production Specialist: Kathy McColley

Library of Congress Cataloging-in-Publication Data
Names: Meister, Cari, author.
Title: Totally wacky facts about YOU! / by Cari Meister.
Other titles: Mind benders (Capstone Press)
Description: North Mankato, Minnesota : Capstone, [2017]
Series: Mind benders | Audience: Ages 8-12. | Audience: Grades 4 to 6.
Identifiers: LCCN 2015031029
ISBN 9781491483763 (paperback)
ISBN 9781491483787 (ebook pdf)
Subjects: LCSH: Human physiology—Miscellanea—Juvenile literature.
Human anatomy—Miscellanea—Juvenile literature. | Brain—Juvenile literature.
Classification: LCC QP37 .M45 2017 | DDC 612—dc23
LC record available at http://lccn.loc.gov/2015031029

Photo Credits

Alamy: The Natural History Museum, 36; Dreamstime: Akulamatiau, 167; Getty Images: Digital Vision, 16; Newscom: Everett Collection, 66 (right), REX/Philip Reeves, 65, Science Photo Library/Steve Gschmeissner, 26-27; Shutterstock: Aaron Amat, 153, advent, 129, Africa Studio, 140 (right), Air Images, 45, Aleks Melnik, 79, Aleksandr Bryliaev, 18, Aleksandr Khakimullin, 191, Alesikka, 42-43, Alexander Pekour, 95, AlexanderZe, 24, Alexandr III, Cover (top left), alphaspirit, 226 (front), Andrei Tarchyshnik, 202, Andrey Armyagov, 25, Aniwhite, 195, Anna Shkolnaya, 166-167, Apollofoto, 111, art_of_sun, 20, ArtHeart, 62, Artishok, 63, Aysezgicmeli, 228, Bard Sandemose, 172, Ben Schonewille, 74, bikeriderlondon, 96, Blamb, 94, blambca, 83 (right), Blend Images, 127, block23, 19, C_Eng-Wong Photography, 80, Carlos Caetano, 43, chikapylka, 107, cobalt88, 226 (back), Complot, 160, Constantine Pankin, 48, Coprid, 104, Cory Thoman, Back Cover, (top right), 177, CREATISTA, 100, Dan Kosmayer, 147, Darren Brode, 15, Daxizo Productions, Cover (top right), 118, Deborah Kolb, 159, dedek, 91, DenisFilm, Cover (bottom right), 205, Designua, 4, Dmitry Kalinovsky, 32, Dooder, 201, DVARG, 142, East, 8 (inset), Ebic, 67, Eldad Carin, 101, EMcgiq, 103, Fabio Berti, 154, Flegere, 124-125, Gala, 188, Gelpi JM, 120, Gencho Petkov, 84, glenda, 140 (left), gosphotodesign, 115, Gun2becontinued, 55, Halfpoint, 123, 198-199, Hardyguardy, 136-137, Haver, 60, HitToon.Com, 86 (right), i3alda, 86 (left), Igor Zh., 158-159, imageerinx, 47, Irina Mir, 92, Ivelin Radkov, 206-207, Iveta Angelova, 183, James Bowyer, 46, Jesada Sabai, 141, Jezper, 97, Jiri Miklo, 37, Jochen Schoenfeld, 6, Johavel, 192, jorgen mcleman, 34, joshya, 5, 88, JPagetRFPhotos, 50, jps, 138, Juan Gaertner, 90, kasahasa, 148-149, Kite_rin, 35, Komsan Loonprom, 2, Konstantin Faraktinov, 75, Konstantin Inozemtsev, 146, Kostiantyn Fastov, 221, koya979, 121, kubais, 12 (bottom), kurhan, 39, lanych, 128, leolintang, 64 (top), Liya Graphics, 58-59, 68, Ljupco Smokovski, 220, 224, lolloj, 178-179, LongQuattro, 152, Lorelyn Medina, 157, lotan, 211, Luis Louro, 72, Lukiyanova Natalia / frenta, 112, Lukutina Olesya, 8 (background), Lyudmyla Kharlamova, 186-187, Macrovector, 130-131, Madlen, 113, 218, Marco Govel, 217, Maridav, 222, Marie Maerz, Cover (bottom left), 207, mart, 108, matimix, 223, Matt Antonio, 87, Matthias G. Ziegler, 203, Maya2008, 53, Monkey Business Images, 117, Monkik, 163, Morphart Creation, 155, murat5234, 64 (bottom), musicman, 181, n_eri, 102, naluwan, 233, Nathalie Spellers Ufermann, 44, NEGOVURA, 116, nemlaza, 60-61, Oksana Shufrych, 230-231, Oleksii Natykach, 81, Orhan Cam, 212, Pagina, 54, Palau, 33, PathDoc, 23, 83 (left), 93, 168, pedalist, 12 (top), Perfect Vectors, 73, Petr Vaclavek, 184-185, Philipp Nicolai, Back Cover, (bottom left), 10, photka, 7, Pinon Road, 69, pio3, 215, Piotr Marcinski, Back Cover (bottom right), 61, 137, Puwadol Jaturawutthichai, 13, ra2studio, 171, Radu Bercan, 41, ratch, 170, RedKoala, 22, Robert Adrian Hillman, 52, Robin Crossman, 105, Rocketclips, Inc, 14, Roman Sigaev, 187, RONORMANJR, 119, Sam72, 132, Samuel Borges Photography, 225, Sanjacm, 173, Sebastian Kaulitzki, 78, Sergey Furtaev, 197, Sergey Korkin, 76, Sergey Shenderovsky, 175, Serova Aleksandra, 74-75, SFerdon, 106, Sheftsoff Women Girls, 229, Shirstok, 164, solarseven, 30-31, SoRad, 162, sss615, 85, sumire8, 139, Suzanne Tucker, 9, 89, TinnaPong, 109, tommaso lizzul, 28, totallyPic.com, 208, Valery Sidelnykov, 125, VIGE.CO, 134 (bottom), Vinicius Tupinamba, 99, Vira Mylyan-Monastyrska, 66 (left), vitstudio, 21, 144-145,vivat, 134 (top), Vladimir Matvienko, 174-175, Volt Collection, 70, Voyagerix, 110, wavebreakmedia, 176, whitehoune, 56-57, www.BillionPhotos.com, 38, Yayayoyo, 98, yomogi1, Back Cover (top left), 11 (inset), yrchello108, 51

Design Elements by Capstone and Shutterstock

Printed in US.
092015   007542CGS16